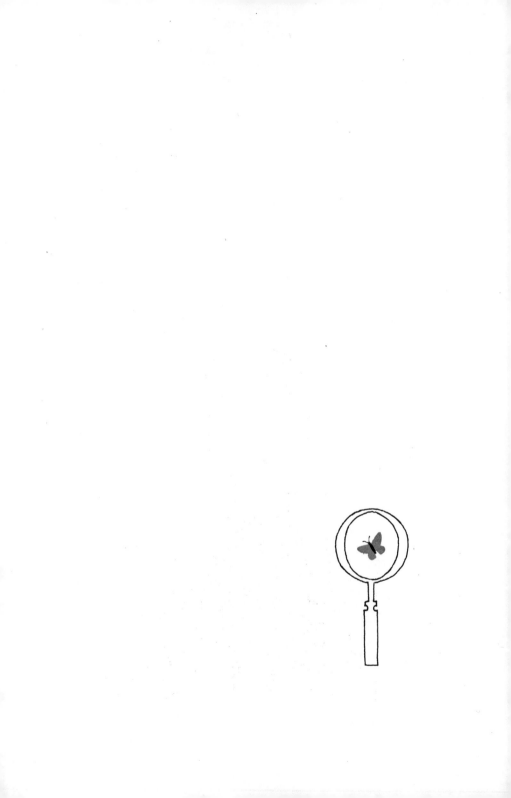

Animals are like this

by Irving Leskowitz
and A. Harris Stone

ILLUSTRATED BY PETER P. PLASENCIA

PRENTICE HALL, INC.   ENGLEWOOD CLIFFS, N. J.

39409

For Martin, Jimmy,
Mandy, and Robin

Third printing........December, 1970

Animals Are Like This by Irving Leskowitz and A. Harris Stone
© 1968 by Irving Leskowitz and A. Harris Stone

Library of Congress Catalog Card Number: 68-13216
Printed in the United States of America
J
Prentice-Hall International, Inc., *London*
Prentice-Hall of Australia, Pty. Ltd., *Sydney*
Prentice-Hall of Canada, Ltd., *Toronto*
Prentice-Hall of India Private Ltd., *New Delhi*
Prentice-Hall of Japan, Inc., *Tokyo*

CONTENTS

INTRODUCTION

This is a book of experiments on animals. Everyone knows, or thinks he knows, what an animal is. If the average person is asked to make a list of animals, he will almost certainly include such animals as dog, cat, horse, lion, elephant, and so on. Some people may remember that birds, snakes and fish are animals, too. A few may even include earthworms and insects. All of these are easily recognized as being animals. But there are some *organisms* that cause difficulty for biologists who try to classify them. In certain ways, these organisms resemble plants; in other ways, they are like animals. They have some characteristics that are "animal characteristics," and others that are "plant characteristics."

There are several ways of tackling the problem of classifying these organisms. One way is to say that they are neither plants nor animals—that they are an entirely different kind of organism. Some biologists have done just this and have classified organisms into three groups— the Plant Kingdom, the Animal Kingdom and the Protista. Other biologists are content to stick to the traditional two groups, the Plant Kingdom and the Animal Kingdom. Most biologists settle this problem by following a simple rule: an animal is any organism that a zoologist says is an animal; a plant is any organism that a botanist says is a plant.

Suppose a botanist and a zoologist both examine one of these troublesome organisms. If they are equally skilled, both will see exactly the same things. Yet one will say the organism is a plant and the other will claim it is an animal. Is one of them right and the other wrong? Not really. Even though both have seen the same things, they may interpret their observations differently. In science, there is usually little argument or disagreement about facts, but there is plenty of room for differences of opinion about the meaning or interpretation of the facts. For instance, muscle contraction is a fact, and all biologists agree that muscle does contract. But there are at least two different schools of thought about what happens inside muscle to make it contract.

One of the characteristics of science is the importance that is placed on getting the facts straight. The scientist must be sure that observations are made and reported accurately because all the work that follows is only as good as the facts on which it is based. On the basis of facts, the scientist tries to explain what he has observed. This is a second characteristic of science: it looks for explanations for events.

Scientists go about their work in a systematic way. Let us suppose that a scientist has observed something happen and wants to find out how it happened. He first guesses what the explanation might be. This guess, or *hypothesis*, must be tested to see whether or not it is correct. The test is an experiment. If the experiment shows the hypothesis to be wrong, the scientist discards the hypothesis and forms a new one. He then designs another experiment to test the new hypothesis. He may discard several hypotheses before he finds one that is supported by experimental results. The results of an experiment make up evidence. When the scientist has gathered enough evidence supporting the hypothesis, he may propose a *theory*. A theory is a statement that explains, in general terms, the relationships among observed facts or events. On the basis of the theory the scientist may make predictions about related events.

A theory is the goal scientists try to achieve, but it is not a final statement. In other words, once a theory is found it does not mean that it will stand forever. Some new observation may be made which cannot be explained by the theory. Then the theory will have to be changed to take into consideration the new information. Scientists know that theories may be useful for a while, but that they may later be shown to be in need of correction. Therefore a scientist treats with respect the theories suggested by other scientists, even though they may disagree with his own.

9

Non-scientists work the same way as scientists, up to a point. The big difference between the scientific way and the non-scientific way is the experiment. Scientists are willing and eager to test their hypotheses. In fact, they are not satisfied unless they can perform experiments that give evidence for or against their hypotheses. Non-scientists generally make guesses but never test them.

This is a book of experiments using animals as the experimental subjects. For most experiments, insects have been selected as the subjects. Frogs, earthworms, fish and water fleas are also used. You may wish to use other animals as well and in most cases this is possible. You may wonder why so many of the experiments use insects rather than mice or guinea pigs. For one thing, there is the matter of cost. Furry animals cost a lot to buy and to feed; insects cost nothing to obtain and almost nothing to feed. Also, when the experiment is finished, there is the problem of either keeping or disposing of the animals. Disposal of insects is no problem at all.

The experiments that follow have been chosen carefully; none of them involves causing pain to the animal. When carrying out experiments on animals, scientists are very careful to avoid even a hint of cruel treatment of the subjects. Pulling the wings or legs off flies is not a scientific experiment; it is cruelty. What can be learned from such an exercise? Nothing useful that could not be learned through a more humane approach.

Now it is time to do some of the experiments. Work carefully, make accurate observations, keep notes. Don't be satisfied with the first answer you find. Repeat the experiment as many times as needed to convince yourself the answer is correct. To help you do the experiments, there is a list of materials and sources in the back of the book.

When you turn this page, be a scientist—experiment!

COLD FLASHES

Does the rate of light flashing in fireflies change? What controls the number of light flashes that a firefly makes in one minute? How does heating or cooling the air surrounding a firefly affect the number of flashes that it produces per minute?

Is the number of times a firefly flashes during one minute the same during the day as at night? (Think carefully—this is a tricky question.) Is there a temperature at which the rate of flashing is greatest?

Firefly flashes have kept many youngsters fascinated for hours and many scientists occupied for years. Fireflies are not the only animals that can give off light. A great many other animals can glow or produce light—certain worms, squid, jellyfish and deep-sea fish can do this. There are even some plants that produce light. The glow or flash that fireflies and other organisms produce is the result of a chemical reaction which releases energy in the form of light. The production of light by animals or plants is called *bioluminescence.* Since little or no heat is produced by bioluminescence, it is also called *cold light.*

Chemical reactions are influenced by many factors, one of the most important being heat. The chemical reaction of bioluminescence is no exception. One convenient thing about this reaction is that it is very simple to tell what effect any factor has on it. If the reaction is speeded by an increase in temperature, for example, the flashes will occur more frequently; if the reaction is slowed, the flashes will occur less frequently. If the temperature increase stops the reaction completely, the flashes will also stop. Because the flashing is quite sensitive to the temperature of the air, it is possible to use fireflies as a sort of thermometer. How accurately can the air temperature be determined if fireflies are used without reference to a thermometer? With a thermometer? Can a formula be found that will allow you to find the temperature without the thermometer? (*Hint:* see Cricket to Cricket.)

FAST FLAPPING

How does the temperature of the air affect the speed at which a butterfly flaps its wings?

A butterfly may be attached to the end of a stick with a drop of quick-drying airplane cement. The butterfly will be easier to handle if it has first been placed in the refrigerator for a short time.

Does the rate at which the wings beat vary with the species of butterfly?

Birds, bats and insects are the only kinds of animals that are able to fly. All of them fly by means of wings powered by muscles. In the case of birds and bats, the wings are constructed of muscle, bone, blood vessels, nerves and skin. Insect wings are quite different. They are simply thin membranes. The muscles moving them are not in the wings at all; they are inside the body. These muscles move the body wall in and out and this, in turn, moves the wings up and down.

Insect flight is remarkable in many ways. For one, many insects can hover in mid-air, like a helicopter. Hummingbirds are the only other animals that can do this. Insects can fly at top speed, stop suddenly in mid-air, and then dart off in any direction.

Large insects with broad wings, such as butterflies and moths, are able to glide and to fly with slow wingbeats. The wingbeat of most insects, however, is very rapid. This speed is responsible for the droning or humming sound of an insect in flight. Each species of insect has its own speed of wingbeat and produces a typical tone. The tone, or note, produced depends upon the speed of the wingbeat, just as the note produced by a tuning fork depends upon the number of vibrations per second. Honeybees' wings beat at the rate of 200 vibrations per second which produces the tone G # below middle C. What note does a housefly produce by its wingbeat? How rapidly do the housefly's wings have to beat to produce that tone? Which insect—mosquito or housefly—has the more rapid wingbeat?

The muscles operating the wings of insects are very much like our own in appearance and function. This is why it is hard to explain how insect wing muscles can contract and relax at such a rapid rate. The best rate that any of our muscles can accomplish is less than 15 contractions per second. Compare this with the 200 or more contractions per second of the honeybee.

Muscle contraction is still not completely understood, but it is known that chemical reaction plays a very important part. The chemical reaction is one that releases a great deal of energy and the reaction is the same in insects as it is in ourselves. This energy is used for muscle contraction. One of the interesting differences, however, between insect muscle contraction and our own muscle contraction is the influence heat has on the rate. In the insect, the rate of the chemical reaction is speeded as the temperature rises. Why does a rise in temperature cause an increase in the rate of insect muscle contraction but not in the rate of muscle contraction in humans?

THE WORM TURNS

What happens to an earthworm's rate of breathing when the temperature of its surroundings changes? How can the rate of breathing be judged? The pellets in the jar are drain cleanser. They absorb a gas that the earthworm gives off when it breathes. What does the oil drop in the straw do when the jar is prepared as shown? What does the motion of the oil drop indicate?

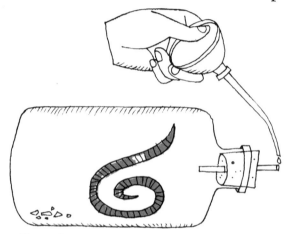

Hint: Allow the jar to remain at room temperature for a few minutes before adding the oil drop to the straw. If the oil drop moves too slowly or not at all, try the experiment with several earthworms in the jar.

Caution: Read the warning printed on the drain cleanser label.

A man can survive without food a week or more and without water for a few days. He can survive only a few minutes without oxygen.

The reason is related to the energy requirements of animals. Man's body consists of billions of tiny units called *cells* together with the products of these cells.

16

(The hard part of bone, the tendons, fingernails, and hair are examples of cell products.) Cells are very active all the time. Some of the activity is easy to see—for instance, muscle cell contraction. Other types of activity are more difficult to detect. Examples of this type are growth and the manufacture of more cell materials. All cell activities require energy. Unless the cell receives energy, it will not be able to carry out any activity at all. Not only that, but the cell needs energy just to keep itself in condition. If cells fail to receive enough energy to maintain themselves, they die.

The energy that animal cells receive comes from food. Inside each cell, chemical reactions take place that break down the food and release energy. The reactions occur in a series: 1 $\longrightarrow$ 2 $\longrightarrow$ 3 $\longrightarrow$ 4 $\rightarrow$ . . . and so on. The final reaction cannot occur unless oxygen is present. If there is no oxygen available, the last reaction does not take place. If this reaction fails to occur, the reaction ahead of it comes to a halt and so on back to the first reaction in the series. In this case, the food would not be broken down, no energy would be released and, in a short while, the cell would die. All the chemical reactions that involve the release of energy make up a process called *respiration.*

As a result of the chemical reactions of respiration, oxygen is used up and carbon dioxide is given off. Therefore, cells must continually be taking in oxygen. Not only that, but they must also get rid of the carbon dioxide since it is poisonous in large amounts. This is what breathing accomplishes for the animal and for cells— it brings oxygen in and removes carbon dioxide. For this reason, most biologists use the word "breathing" to mean an exchange of gases—oxygen in and carbon dioxide out.

HAVE A HEART!

The heartbeat of a daphnid, or water flea, can be seen by looking at the animal through a low-power microscope. This small animal can be held in place by putting it on a bit of petroleum jelly on the bottom of a dish. The daphnid should not be allowed to dry up. What happens to the heartbeat when the daphnid is covered with warm water? With cold water?

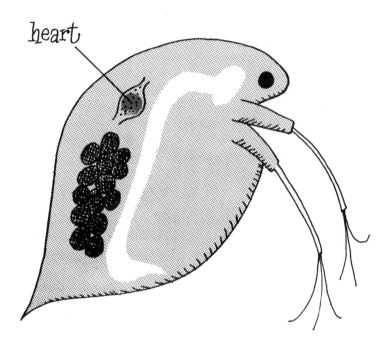

heart

How is the temperature of the water related to the number of heartbeats per minute?

Although no one yet knows why heart muscle beats rhythmically, it *is* known that the heartbeat is affected

18

by many factors such as heat, exercise and certain chemicals. The heart of a daphnid is a good subject for this kind of study since it is very sensitive and is easily visible in a living daphnid.

The heartbeat rate is usually rapid. Here is a hint that will help you count the beats accurately. Have someone keep time while you observe the heartbeat. Tap a pencil point on a sheet of paper in time with the heartbeat. Have the timekeeper count off 15 seconds. The number of pencil marks made in 15 seconds multiplied by four gives the number of heartbeats per minute.

Exactly what degree of heat can a daphnid stand before its heart stops beating? What is the minimum temperature at which its heart still beats?

CRICKET TO CRICKET

How do crickets react to changes in temperature? What is the difference between the number of sounds per minute made by a cricket on a cool day and the number per minute on a warm day?

What happens if, after the cricket sound stops, you make a sound by rubbing a pencil over the teeth of a comb? Does the cricket "talk" while you are making this noise? Are there other sounds that crickets will "answer"?

Do crickets "talk" to one another? Before answering this question, another question must be asked: Can insects hear? There is no doubt that many insects can produce sounds, but biologists are not at all sure that all insects can hear.

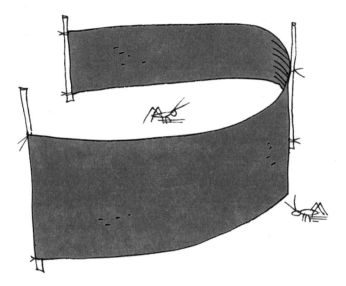

If you can capture two male crickets or grasshoppers of the same species, and place them near one another you can test their ability to hear. Do both *stridulate,* or make noise, at the same time? Do they take turns?

Can crickets tell the temperature? They could if they were able to tell time and add. Here's how:

Number of chirps made in 15 seconds + 40 = the temperature in °F.

PERFUME FOR FLIES

Can fruit flies follow a scent? In what direction will fruit flies go if they are placed in the jars shown here? Does their flight pattern change if the banana in one jar is moved to a different jar?

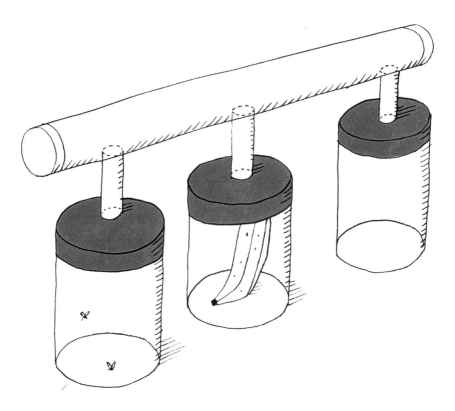

Will changing the kind of food in the jar change the flight path of the flies? How long does it take for the flies to start flying?

The ability to identify odors is of great importance to many animals. In man, this ability is not nearly as well developed as it is in most other animals with a sense of smell. Many animals rely more on their sense of smell than on any other sense, including sight and hearing.

Insects distinguish between friend and foe by odor. If male moths or butterflies are deprived of their *olfactory*, or odor detection, structures they are unable to find the females of their species. Ants do not bother members of their own colony but attack individuals from other ant colonies. If the olfactory organs of an ant are removed, the ant will not only attack ants from other colonies, but ants from its own colony as well.

Insects have no noses—so how are they able to smell? Ants smell with their antennae as do moths, butterflies, cockroaches and many other insects. The antennae are probably not the only olfactory structures. It is believed that in some insects mouth parts and feet may also be able to detect odors.

How sensitive are the olfactory structures of insects? Place a slice of pear or banana out in the open and see how long it takes for insects to find it. The time is more likely to be minutes than hours.

It is known that female moths produce an odorous substance that attracts the male. How might this knowledge be used in pest control?

WHAT DOES IT TASTE LIKE?

Can all substances be tasted on all parts of a person's tongue? What happens if a drop of vinegar is carefully touched to the end of a person's tongue? To the top-center of the tongue? To the sides?

Use salt, sugar and lemon peel to find out which part of the tongue detects each taste. (*Note:* rinse out your mouth after each different substance is tested.)

24

Are odor and taste related? How do foods taste when you have a bad cold? Do they taste the same hot as they do cold? When does a food give off a stronger odor—when it is hot or when it is cold?

The sense of taste is a complex one. There are only four basic tastes that humans can distinguish: sweet, salt, sour and bitter. But there are many more flavors in food than just these four. The many different flavors are made up of various combinations of the four basic tastes plus smell plus texture (smooth, dry, pulpy).

How many senses do animals have? Most people would say "five"—sight, hearing, touch, taste and smell—but they would be wrong. Can you tell when something is hot? Can you tell when you are off-balance or upside down? Have you ever cut your finger or had a splinter under your skin? Each of these sensations involves a different sense.

In order to survive, an animal must be able to receive information from its environment. In other words, animals must know what's happening around them. They find out what they must know by means of various special structures. These structures are called *sensory organs*, or *receptors*. Each different type of receptor responds to, or picks up, a particular kind of *stimulus* and is named accordingly. Here is a list of receptor types. What kind of stimulus does each pick up?

Photoreceptor	Statoreceptor
Phonoreceptor	Thermoreceptor
Chemoreceptor	Pain receptor
Tangoreceptor	

Distributed over four areas of the tongue and on the roof of the mouth are taste receptors called *taste buds*. What type of receptor is a taste bud? What type of receptor is the eye?

WHICH WAY DID THEY GO?

Is it true that you can catch more flies with honey than you can with vinegar? Do other food substances such as lemon juice or butter attract flies?

How would you find out which foods and flavors flies are attracted to?

The importance of the sense of smell is shown by the fact that flies will be attracted to honey but not to sugar water, even if the sugar water is sweeter than the honey. Does honey have an odor? Does sugar water have an odor? Which foods or liquids in the dishes attracted the most flies? Do all these foods have an odor? Do the foods that did not attract flies have an odor? Judging by the number of flies around each food, can you tell which food has the strongest and which has the weakest odor? Some care must be taken in answering these questions because several possibilities must be considered.

One possibility might be that flies are attracted by the sight of other flies. Suppose there are two foods, A and B, close to one another. A fly accidentally finds A and settles down on it, even though B is more fragrant and tasty. Other flies may see the first one on A and join it there, ignoring B.

A second possibility is that flies bring about changes in the odor of foods as they feed. Flies do not have biting mouth parts. They cannot take in solid food. But we have all seen flies on slices of fruit or bread and these are certainly solid foods. How do flies eat these foods? When a fly has tasted something that appeals to it, it deposits a small drop of saliva on the food. The saliva contains enzymes that digest the food and change it chemically. Some of the products of the digestion may then produce odors that attract other flies.

How could an experiment be designed to show which possibility is correct? Are there other explanations that may fit? What experimental controls are necessary when doing these studies?

TOUCH AND TASTE

How is a butterfly able to know the difference between food and things that are not food? What happens to a butterfly's proboscis when its antennae are touched with cotton soaked in a sugar solution? What happens to the proboscis when the butterfly's feet are touched with the sugared cotton? Are certain of its feet more sensitive than others?

Is the reaction stronger if the butterfly is not allowed to eat for one day before the experiment is done?

The sense of taste and the sense of smell both depend upon receptors called *chemoreceptors*. These are structures that are able to detect chemicals. Both taste and smell involve the ability to recognize chemicals.

Most animals have no nose but do have different kinds of olfactory organs. These olfactory organs include antennae, mouth parts and others. In some animals, certain structures may serve as both odor and taste receptors, while other structures may serve for one or the other, but not both. The antennae of certain insects have receptors for odor, taste, touch and perhaps other stimuli. Flies, bees, butterflies and some other insects have taste receptors located in the foot joints. They are also able to taste by means of specialized mouth parts. Having taste receptors on the feet is very useful for these insects. In walking about, their feet come into contact with many different substances. As soon as they step on something that has an appealing taste, they begin their feast. This kind of taste test is quick, easy and safe. It is not necessary for such an insect to take substances into its mouth in order to find out whether or not it should eat it.

Observe a fly as it walks about. Notice that it stops frequently to rub its legs together and clean them. This procedure is probably the fly's way of keeping its taste receptors in working condition.

Mix some food coloring, sugar and water and smear the mixture on a sheet of paper. After some flies have found it, there should be a nice set of footprints and mouthprints on the paper.

A MATTER OF TASTE

Test a butterfly's ability to taste sugar against a person's ability. How sensitive is the butterfly's taste for sweetness compared with that of a person?

What is the weakest sugar solution to which the butterfly responds? Is the least concentrated sugar solution that a butterfly can detect stronger or weaker than the least concentrated solution a person can taste?

Set up a series of sugar dilutions. Which one has the minimum concentration below which a sweet taste cannot be detected? Call it solution A. Hold a little bit of concentrated sugar solution in your mouth for a minute or two. Rinse your mouth quickly with fresh water, then taste solution A again. Can a sweet taste be detected?

This experiment shows two characteristics of receptors. One is sensitivity. A receptor is unable to detect a stimulus unless the stimulus is strong enough. For example, a sound receptor cannot detect a sound unless the sound is loud enough. Taste receptors cannot detect the taste of a substance unless there is enough of that substance present. The minimum amount or strength of a stimulus that is able to cause a receptor to respond is called the *threshold*.

The second characteristic of receptors that the experiment showed was *fatigue*. To illustrate this, place some perfume in one dish and a little bit of a different perfume in a second dish. Smell the first perfume. How long does it take before its odor can no longer be noticed? Immediately, smell the second perfume. Can its odor be detected? After a minute or two, smell the first perfume again. Can its odor now be detected? If a strong stimulus is applied to a receptor for a long enough time, the receptor no longer responds. The reason for this is not clearly understood. Some biologists think the receptor just becomes tired or fatigued from overwork. Others say the receptors become accustomed to the stimulus and no longer respond. Whatever the explanation, the receptor doesn't respond. But this condition, as you have seen, is temporary. After a short rest, the receptor is as good as new.

TASTE CONFUSION

Is it possible to confuse the tasting ability of a butter-fly? Can a butterfly tell the difference between a sugar solution and a salt solution? What happens when a butterfly tastes a sugar solution to which salt has been added?

What effect is seen if a saccharine solution is used in place of the sugar solution? Does the butterfly respond in the same way to sugars other than common table sugar?

Insects have a very keen sense of taste. They are able to taste extremely small amounts of certain substances. Just how insects taste foods is not known in all details. Most *entomologists* believe that the taste sense of insects probably functions in the same way as that of any other animal. The sense of taste, like the sense of smell, is a chemical sense. That is, it depends upon a chemoreceptor. Chemoreceptors are stimulated when they come into contact with certain substances. However, if the explanation of the sense of taste were as simple as this, there would be little mystery surrounding the question of how it works. What makes the investigation of taste receptors so fascinating to biologists is that a given type of taste receptor will respond only to a given substance or type of substance and not to any other. At least, this is true so far as humans are concerned. It is not known whether or not it is true for other animals.

The reaction of the butterfly's proboscis shows that the butterfly can taste very small concentrations of sugar. It has been seen that some insects can taste the same substances humans can. Some of these seem to be as objectionable to the insects as they are to humans. On the other hand, there are some substances that humans can taste that appear to be tasteless to insects.

The same sort of differences in ability to taste can be found among humans. There is a substance called *phenylthiocarbamide,* PTC for short, that many people cannot taste at all. But to some people it has a salty taste, to some a bitter taste, to others a sweet taste, and to still others a sour taste. The way PTC tastes to a person is based on a hereditary factor and the taste reaction to this substance usually runs in families. Why one particular substance should have a different taste to different people is a problem that has not yet been solved.

IT'S A GAS!

What happens when bubbles are blown through water containing some phenolphthalein? Does the color change depend on how long the bubbles continue to be blown through the solution?

What happens to the color of the solution if a piece of raw liver is placed in it? Can the color change be reversed? What happens if an insect is sealed in a test tube with some phenolphthalein solution?

Note: Prepare the phenolphthalein solution as follows: Add 3 to 5 drops of phenolphthalein to some water in a glass. If the water remains colorless, add to it, drop by drop, a solution of sodium bicarbonate in water. Stir the solution after each drop. Stop when a pink color appears and remains, even after stirring.

Animals breathe in oxygen from the atmosphere and breathe out carbon dioxide. There are many ways this exchange of gases may be shown. One way makes use of substances like sodium hydroxide, the main ingredient in drain cleansers. Such substances absorb, or take up carbon dioxide. This is the method used in an earlier experiment. Another method takes advantage of substances called *indicators*. As the name tells us, indicators are substances that indicate or tell something. What they indicate is whether a solution is an acid, a base or neither. Indicators are able to do this because they change color depending upon the condition of the solution. For example, an indicator called brom thymol blue is blue when the solution is alkaline or neutral. As the solution is made more and more acidic, brom thymol blue changes color from blue to blue-green to green to greenish-yellow and finally to yellow. Another indicator, phenolphthalein, is red when the solution is very alkaline, changes to pink and then becomes colorless as the solution becomes more acidic.

Like many gases, carbon dioxide can dissolve in water. When it does so, the carbon dioxide combines with the water to form a weak acid called carbonic acid. As you breathe out through the straw, you are bubbling carbon dioxide through the water and this results in the formation of carbonic acid, making the solution more acidic. If an indicator, such as phenolphthalein were present, the change in color would show this.

DON'T HOLD YOUR BREATH

By carefully watching a frog in a jar, it is possible to count the number of breaths the frog takes per minute. What happens to the breathing rate if the jar containing the frog is partially filled with carbon dioxide?

Carbon dioxide can be produced by adding water to baking powder.

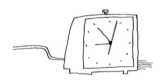

Some children try to get their own way by threatening to hold their breath until they die. Can a person hold his breath that long? Can a person control his breathing just by wanting to? If so, how can we explain the fact that people breathe even when they are asleep and not thinking about it?

There are two types of muscle control in animals. One is called *involuntary* because the muscles involved carry out their action whether or not the animal wishes it. The other type of control is called *voluntary*. Signing your name, jumping, turning your head—all of these are examples of the kind of muscle activity under voluntary control. The muscles act only when you want them to.

The muscles involved in breathing are unusual in that both sets of controls, voluntary and involuntary, play a part. We can make ourselves breathe more deeply or breathe more rapidly. We can hold our breath for short periods. These represent breathing actions under voluntary control. Normally we breathe without thinking about it. This is involuntary.

What is involved in the involuntary control? There is a small part of the brain that is called the breathing center. The breathing center sends messages to the muscles that are responsible for inhaling and exhaling. It works day and night, asleep or awake, and we are never aware of it. When the breathing center is stimulated, it sends the messages out more rapidly, causing a speedup in the breathing rate. When it is not stimulated, the breathing center sends out messages slowly, causing a slowdown in the breathing rate.

The next question is, What stimulates the breathing center? One of the factors is carbon dioxide and it acts in an intricate way. The more actively muscles work, the more oxygen they need and the more carbon dioxide they produce. The carbon dioxide is a waste product and is removed from the muscles by the bloodstream. Therefore, as the muscles work harder and faster, the amount of carbon dioxide in the blood increases. Any increase in the amount of carbon dioxide stimulates the breathing center in the brain and increases the breathing rate. This, in turn, means that the carbon dioxide is removed faster and that more oxygen is carried to the muscles.

If a person holds his breath long enough, the carbon dioxide is not breathed out and accumulates in the blood. The accumulation stimulates the breathing center more and more strongly until finally the involuntary muscles act and the person breathes whether he wants to or not.

MAKING MOISTURE

What change can be seen in a piece of cobalt chloride paper if it is hung in a small corked bottle containing some flies? A bottle containing some other insect?

Does changing the temperature of the air in the bottle by placing the bottle in a pan of warm water have any effect on the speed of what is observed?

The energy reactions involved in respiration produce carbon dioxide and water as waste products. Carbon dioxide is eliminated by breathing. Water is eliminated in various ways, depending upon the kind of animal. One way water is given off in air-breathing animals, such as humans, is by breathing. Insects also are air-breathing animals and therefore excrete water by breathing. Does the experiment show anything about breathing out moisture?

Cobalt chloride is a substance that is an indicator. Instead of indicating whether a solution is acid or alkaline, however, cobalt chloride indicates whether or not moisture is present. You may have seen the novelty "weather forecaster" cards. If they turn pink, it means that it may rain; if they turn blue, fair weather is on the way. These weather forecasters contain cobalt chloride. Cobalt chloride is a salt that is blue when dry and pink when moist.

Can a strip of cobalt chloride paper help show if there is any moisture in the air you breathe in? In the air you exhale?

Do you breathe more rapidly when the temperature is high than you do when it is low? Why should insects breathe more rapidly as the temperature rises? The answers to these questions are helpful to an understanding of an important division in the animal kingdom. There are two large groups of animals. The animals of one group become more active as the temperature rises. Animals of the other group are not affected by the temperature in this way. They may be just as active at high temperatures as they are at low temperatures. Animals of the second group are commonly called "warm-blooded." Only birds and mammals belong to this group. All other animals—insects, worms, fish, reptiles, amphibians—are called "cold-blooded" animals. Biologists do not use the terms "warm-blooded" and "cold-blooded" because the words may be misleading. "Cold-blooded" animals may, at times, have very warm blood, depending upon the temperature of their surroundings. In fact, it is just this point that is meaningful. The body temperature of a "cold-blooded" animal changes with the temperature of its surroundings. A "warm-blooded" animal has a body temperature that does not vary by more than a degree or two no matter what the temperature of the environment may be.

Since the body temperature of "warm-blooded" animals remains constant, the chemical reactions taking place in the body continue to occur at the same rate. If a "cold-blooded" animal is placed in a cold environment, its body temperature will be lowered and the chemical reactions will be slowed down. The reverse will be true if the animal is placed in a warm environment.

THE WORM RETURNS

How does the nature of the liquid that an earthworm passes through affect the earthworm? Do earthworms prefer solutions that are sweet? Salty? Are there any liquids or solutions that earthworms appear to dislike? How can you tell if an earthworm "likes" or "dislikes" a solution?

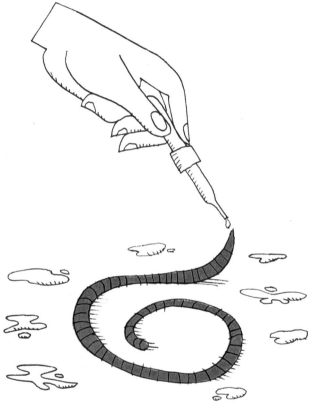

Try using fruit juices, vinegar, soda water, and other liquids.

Note: Earthworm should be placed on a rough surface.

The two types of chemoreceptors that humans have are located in the nasal passages and on the tongue. Insects have taste and odor receptors on their feet and on their mouth parts. Some biologists suspect that insects have additional taste and odor receptors located on other parts of their bodies. Many animals that do not have mouth parts, feet or noses, are able to detect chemical stimuli. The chemical receptors in some of these animals are located in the skin or outer body covering. In many cases these receptors have not been seen and identified, but since the animals show a definite response to chemicals, it is believed that the receptors must be present.

Which portion of the earthworm's body is most sensitive to chemical stimuli—front, middle or rear? Does the earthworm have a top and bottom? Are both top and bottom equally sensitive to chemical stimuli?

Is the earthworm responding to the chemical or is it responding to being touched? How can you tell which is the case? In any experiment, a control is needed. The control is a procedure that allows the experimenter to decide whether the results are due to the factors being tested or whether the same results would have been obtained even if that factor had not been used. What would the control be in this experiment?

What type of experiment would show whether or not a butterfly has chemoreceptors on parts of its body other than its feet and mouth?

ANT TRAILS

How do ants find their way from place to place? What will an ant do if it comes across a trail of sugar solution? What will the ant do if a trail of salt solution is made across the sugar trail?

What will an ant do if it is placed at the end of a sugar trail crossed by five or six different trails? Try vinegar, coffee, salad oil and other kitchen liquids to make these different trails. Make a trail with a dilute solution of formic acid. Which trail appears to have the strongest attraction for ants?

Anyone who has seen ants following each other along a trail must have wondered how they stay on the trail. It almost seems as though the ants are following road signs. At one end of the trail is the entrance to the ant nest. At the other end of the trail is usually a piece of food.

The method ants use to follow trails depends upon the species of ant. Some ant species navigate by the sun, taking their directions from its position in the sky. There is some evidence that certain insects, including ants, guide themselves by the light in the sky without even seeing the sun. They can find their way quite accurately even on cloudy, overcast days. It has been found that they guide themselves by the polarization of light in the sky.

Find a trail and observe the ants as they move along it. The traffic pattern they make is like that of a two-way street. Very few ants stray off the path. What do ants do if they accidentally stray off the path? What does an ant do if someone pushes it off the path? Can the ant find the path again? Can any of the trail-making substances used in this experiment be used to fool ants? If so, which substance works best?

Many species of ants follow scent trails. What happens if a section of an ant path is removed by brushing or shoveling it away? Can the path be restored artifically? What substance is given off by ants to mark their trails?

Hint: The Latin name for the ant family is Formicoidea.

TAILS OF TWO FISH

The blood in an animal flows through small tube-like structures. This flow can be seen by looking at the thinnest part of a fish tail through a hand magnifying glass or a microscope. To keep a fish alive while watching its blood circulate, wrap it in wet cloth.

Compare the rates of blood flow in the fish tails treated as shown below. What happens if strong tea or coffee is used in place of alcohol?

Three hundred years ago it was believed that the blood flowed to the outer parts of the body through both arteries and veins. After reaching the outer portions of the body, the blood was then thought to flow back through the same blood vessels to the heart and liver. In other words, people in the sixteenth century believed that the blood ebbed and flowed like the tide. A given blood vessel could carry blood in one direction one moment and in the opposite direction the next. This idea, which had been believed for hundreds of years, was shown to be wrong by an English physician named William Harvey. His experiments showed that blood vessels were one-way streets and that the blood must flow in one continuous direction through the body. Although he never saw them, he predicted that there must be smaller blood vessels connecting arteries and veins. Harvey stated that the blood must flow in one direction only: from the heart through arteries through smaller vessels to veins and then back to the heart. Marcello Malpighi, an Italian scientist, later discovered the small blood vessels running from arteries to veins. These vessels are called *capillaries*. There are many thousands of them per square inch of skin.

Are capillaries sensitive to heat, cold and chemicals? Why does the skin turn red when it is burned or scalded?

Some chemicals cause blood vessels to *constrict,* or become narrower. Other chemicals cause blood vessels to *dilate,* or become wider. If a vessel is constricted, what happens to the rate of blood flow through it? Is alcohol a *vasoconstrictor* or a *vasodilator?*

THE DRUNKEN DAPHNID

What happens to the daphnid's heartbeat when a small amount of instant coffee is added to the water? When still more coffee is added?

Replace the coffee with fresh water.

Try adding some alcohol to the water. What happens?

Make a nicotine solution by grinding up some cigarette tobacco in water. Add a drop or two of nicotine solution to fresh water containing a daphnid and count heartbeats again.

Note: Prepare for this in advance by filling a jar with tap water and allowing it to stand in the open for 2 or 3 days. Use this water for all parts of this experiment.

The heart is really a blood vessel. True, it is larger, thicker, stronger, more complicated and more active than any other blood vessel. During the development and growth of an animal embryo, the blood vessels are formed almost at the start. Later, a special section of a large blood vessel becomes more muscular and eventually forms the heart. Since the heart starts as a blood vessel, it behaves very much like other blood vessels. Therefore it should respond to chemicals in much the same way capillaries do. Is alcohol a stimulant or a depressant? What about coffee and tea?

HEALTHY, IT'S NOT!

What happens to flies in a glass jar if cigarette smoke is drawn through the jar? Do the flies "recover" after they are released from the jar following the smoke treatment?

Ask an adult who smokes for help with this one!

What is the effect of cigarette smoke on ants, cockroaches or other insects? How long does it take for the smoke to affect each kind of insect?

What effects can be seen when different brands of cigarettes are used? Different lengths? Filters and non-filters? Pipes? Cigars? Lettuce cigarettes?

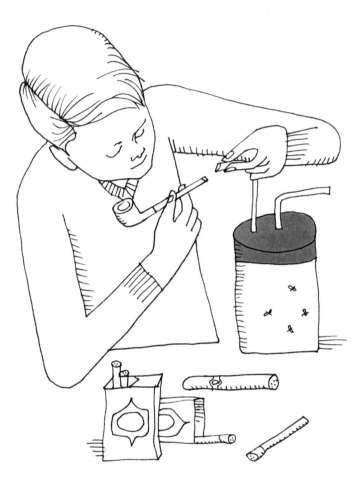

49

THE LIGHT AND THE DARK

How do daphnids in water react to a strong flashlight beam? Does the addition of a little soda water change the daphnid's reaction to light?

Try this in a darkened room as well as in a light one.

The subject of animal behavior is of interest to both biologists and psychologists. Each group's interest, however, involves different circumstances. The psychologists want to know what effects outside conditions have on what animals do and on how animals learn and solve problems. Biologists are interested in the same things but are more concerned with learning how the behavior of animals is dependent upon physiological factors. The questions psychologists ask might be: "What will an animal do if the conditions are such and such?" or "What factors influence the ability of an animal to learn?" A biologist, on the other hand, might ask "What physiological or metabolic activity is responsible for a particular kind of behavior?"

There are at least three different types of animal behavior: *taxis, instinct* and *reasoning.* The simplest type of behavior is called a taxis. This action is found among less complex animals, such as the one-celled *protozoa.* A taxis is a response that is specific for a given condition. For example, planaria (an animal of the type called flatworms) avoids strong light. If a strong light is beamed on it, planaria will always move away from the light. This kind of response is called a *negative phototaxis.* If the animal had moved toward the light, the response would be called a *positive phototaxis.*

A taxis really is not quite as simple as it appears to be. Biologists still do not know as much as they would like to about this type of behavior. In fact, there is still no complete and satisfactory explanation for the response to light of a daphnid in an acid solution.

ANIMAL ENZYMES

A solution of animal enzymes can be obtained by grinding a piece of fresh liver in some water and straining the mixture. The liquid that comes through the strainer contains enzymes. What happens if a few drops of this liquid are added to some hydrogen peroxide? Does adding plain water to hydrogen peroxide give the same effect?

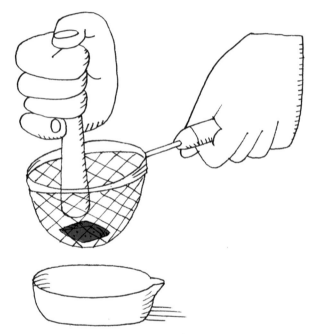

How long does the effect last? Does adding more enzyme solution renew the effect? Does adding more hydrogen peroxide change what is seen?

Many chemical reactions occur so rapidly that they result in an explosion. Other reactions take place very slowly and require hours or even days for the products to be formed. Sometimes the speed of a reaction can be very important. For instance, nylon is manufactured by means of a relatively slow chemical reaction. If nothing were done to speed the reaction, it would take a very long time to produce the amount of nylon the manufacturer would like. In the production of nylon, a substance is added to the chemical mixture that speeds the reaction and brings it to completion more rapidly.

There are many substances that have this ability to increase the rate of reactions. These substances are called *catalysts*. Another property of catalysts is that they are not used up during the reaction. At the end of the reaction, there is just as much catalyst left as there was at the beginning.

In the body of an animal, thousands upon thousands of chemical reactions take place every minute. Some of these reactions make food available and ready for body use; other reactions supply energy to the body. If such reactions took a long time to complete, the animal might starve to death on a full stomach or die for lack of energy. This does not happen, of course, because the reactions in animal bodies take place in seconds or fractions of a second. The speed of chemical reactions in animals is due to the activity of enzymes. Enzymes are catalysts of a very special nature. First, they are produced only by living things. Second, they are extremely active, even in very small amounts. Third, they are *specific* for particular reactions. For example, there is one enzyme which speeds up only the reaction in which hydrogen peroxide is changed into water and oxygen. This enzyme is called catalase and is found in many plants and animals. Catalase does not work as a catalyst for any other reaction.

INHALE, EXHALE

Are fireflies able to flash if there is more carbon dioxide in the air than usual?

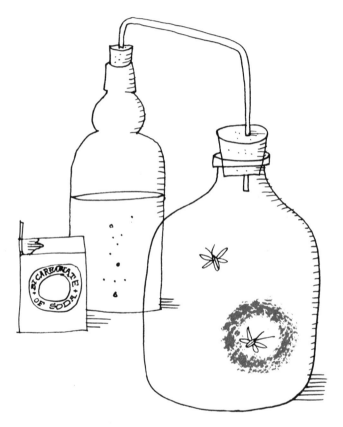

Does "flooding" the air in the jar with oxygen have any effect on the flashing?

Hint: Oxygen can be produced by dropping a piece of raw liver into hydrogen peroxide.

Fireflies are one of the most widely used subjects for research on bioluminescence. Other good subjects are jellyfish, shrimp and certain bacteria. Light is produced in much the same way in all of these different organisms.

One question that scientists ask about bioluminescence is "In what way, if any, is the light useful to the organisms that produce it?" In some cases, the answer is obvious. Certain worms living in the ocean are able to locate each other at mating time by means of the flashes they produce. The same is true of fireflies. Some deep-sea fish, such as the angler fish, have a "lantern" that lures their prey within striking distance. But there are many organisms that produce light and seem to have no use for it. For example, certain jellyfish and certain bacteria produce light, but have no way of detecting light. They are capable of sending out light signals but cannot see the signals sent out by others.

One of the early experimenters noted that if the light-producing organs of a firefly are ground up, they still produce light. If the tube containing the organs was put into hot water, no light was produced. The chemical reaction of light production is one that involves an *enzyme*. Does this explain the effect of temperature on the reaction?

The enzyme is one of the keys to the reaction. This was shown by another experiment that was done. The firefly substance that glows is called luciferin. The enzyme needed for the light-producing reaction is called *luciferase*. There are two groups of fireflies in North America—*Photuris* and *Photinus*. The experiment was as follows:

luciferin + luciferase from *Photuris* $\longrightarrow$ yellow light
luciferin + luciferase from *Photinus* $\longrightarrow$ orange light

It was found that the reaction only worked if luciferin, luciferase and one other substance were mixed. What is that other substance?

ENZYME CONCENTRATION

How does varying the amount of an enzyme in a solution affect the action of the enzyme? The chart below will serve as a guide for this experiment. Be patient when doing this one; it's not easy!

EFFECT OF ENZYME CONCENTRATION ON ACTIVITY

Trial #	Amount of hydrogen peroxide	Amount of enzyme solution	Amount of water	Time for bubbling to stop
1	10 drops	1 drop	9 drops	?
2	10 drops	2 drops	8 drops	?
3	10 drops	4 drops	6 drops	?
4	10 drops	7 drops	3 drops	?
5	10 drops	10 drops	0	?
6	1 drop	5 drops	4 drops	?
7	2 drops	5 drops	3 drops	?
8	3 drops	5 drops	2 drops	?
9	4 drops	5 drops	1 drop	?
10	5 drops	5 drops	0	?

Enzymes are unlike other kinds of catalysts in many ways. One difference between enzymes and other types of catalysts is that the enzymes are far more sensitive to conditions such as temperature, acidity or alkalinity, and the presence of certain other substances.

All of these will affect the rate of enzyme activity. There are many ways in which the rate of a reaction may be determined. The easiest kind of reaction to measure is one that produces a visible change, such as a change in color, when the reaction is completed. Another easy type is one that produces gas bubbles. When the reaction is complete, the bubbling stops.

For a given concentration of *substrate,* does varying the concentration of enzyme have any effect on the rate of the reaction? The substance upon which an enzyme acts is called the *substrate.* In this case, the enzyme is catalase; the substrate is hydrogen peroxide.

For a given concentration of enzyme, does varying the concentration of substrate have any effect on the rate of the reaction? Is there a specific combination of substrate concentration and enzyme concentration that causes the fastest rate?

ENZYMES, ACIDS AND BASES

What effect do acids and bases have on the action of the enzyme catalase? The chart (p. 59) tells you how to set up this experiment. (A set of directions of this sort for an experiment is called an *experimental protocol*. It is one way a scientist plans his work for any experiment.)

Chemists have a shorthand way of describing whether a solution is an acid or a base. They refer to the *pH* of a solution. The pH is measured in numbers from 1 to 14. A solution that has a pH of 7 is neutral; it is neither acidic nor basic. Below pH 7, the solution is acid; solutions with a pH above 7 are alkaline or basic. The lower the pH, the more acid the solution; pH 1 is the most acid any solution can be. The higher the pH, the more alkaline the solution; pH 14 is the most alkaline any solution can be.

The pH of a solution is very important for enzyme action. Some enzymes work best at a basic pH, others work best at an acid pH and still others work best at pH 7 or close to it. For each enzyme there is a particular pH at which that enzyme works best.

EFFECT OF pH ON CATALASE ACTIVITY

Trial #	Amount of enzyme solution	Amount of hydrogen peroxide	Amount of acid (vinegar)	Amount of base (bicarbonate of soda solution)	Amount of water	Time for bubbling to stop
1	5 drops	10 drops	10 drops	0	0	?
2	5 drops	10 drops	7 drops	0	3 drops	?
3	5 drops	10 drops	5 drops	0	5 drops	?
4	5 drops	10 drops	3 drops	0	7 drops	?
5	5 drops	10 drops	0	0	10 drops	?
6	5 drops	10 drops	0	10 drops	0	?
7	5 drops	10 drops	0	7 drops	3 drops	?
8	5 drops	10 drops	0	5 drops	5 drops	?
9	5 drops	10 drops	0	3 drops	7 drops	?
10	5 drops	10 drops	0	0	10 drops	?

Which trials should give the same results? Which trials are the control?

59

GLOSSARY

BIOLUMINESCENCE—the production of light by an organism. The chemical reaction producing the light gives off no heat; for this reason, bioluminescence is also called *cold light*. The organisms that produce cold light include bacteria, mushrooms, protozoa, jellyfish, worms, squid, shrimp, insects and many fish.

CAPILLARY—a very small, thin-walled blood vessel. Capillaries bring blood into close contact with all the tissues of the body. Arteries branch successively to form smaller and smaller vessels. The smallest of these are the capillaries. Capillaries join to form veins. The flow of blood through the body is from heart through arteries through capillaries through veins back to the heart.

CATALYST—a substance that speeds the rate of a chemical reaction. The catalyst itself does not undergo chemical change and does not take part in the reaction. As a result, it is not used up; at the end of the reaction, there is present the same amount of catalyst as there was at the beginning. The catalyst may therefore be used over and over again.

CHEMORECEPTOR—a sense organ specialized to receive and respond to chemical stimuli. Taste buds and olfactory organs are the chemoreceptors responsible for taste detection and odor detection respectively.

ENTOMOLOGIST—a scientist who specializes in the study of insects.

GERMICIDE—any chemical that kills "germs," or harmful microorganisms. Such products as mouthwashes, antiseptics, and disinfectants are, or contain, germicides.

INDICATOR—a chemical that changes color as the pH of its solution changes. The color of the indicator is always the same for a given degree of acidity or alkalinity. Each indicator has a particular pH range over which it is useful. Brom cresol purple, for example, is effective from pH 5.2 to pH 6.8. At the more acid lower end of its range, brom cresol purple is yellow; at the upper end, which is near neutrality, the indicator is purple. At any pH between 5.2 and 6.8, brom cresol purple has a characteristic color. At pH's less than 5.2, there is no further color change—the indicator remains yellow. Similarly, there is no further color change at pH's above 6.8.

INHIBITOR—a substance that prevents the normal action of an enzyme. Inhibitors are effective only as long as they are in contact with the enzyme. Their effect is temporary; once the inhibitor is removed, the enzyme is just as efficient as ever. Many inhibitors are specific for particular enzymes and have no effect on other enzymes.

INSTINCT—a behavior pattern that consists of a chain of set responses. Each response, or action, is triggered by the action preceding it. The entire series of responses is inflexible; a given stimulus will start a chain of responses that never vary. Some instinctive responses are relatively simple; others are highly complex and involve the interaction of two individuals.

OLFACTORY—refers to the sense of smell.

ORGANISM—any living individual, whether plant, animal or protist.

pH—a symbol used by scientists to tell the degree of acidity or alkalinity of a solution. A solution that is neither acidic nor alkaline is called neutral and its pH is 7.0. Solutions with a pH less than 7.0 are acidic; the lower the pH, the more strongly acid is the solution. Alkaline solutions have pH's greater than 7.0; the higher the pH, the more strongly alkaline is the solution. The values of pH range from 1.0 to 14.0.

PHOTORECEPTOR—a sense organ specialized to receive and respond to light.

PROTISTA—a category of organisms. It was established to include those organisms that do not fit neatly into either the plant or animal kingdoms. Such organisms as bacteria, molds and protozoa, among others, are classified as protists.

STATORECEPTOR—a receptor for the sense of equilibrium. In most animals, the statoreceptors are located in the head; in some they are located in the antennae. In humans, two statoreceptors are parts of the inner ear.

STIMULUS—any change, either inside the body of an animal or in its external environment, that causes a receptor to respond. Sights, sounds, odors, and so on are stimuli. Change in position, such as a loss of balance, may also be a stimulus.

STRIDULATION—the production of a grating sound, accomplished by certain insects by rubbing together certain parts of the body. In some insects, stridulation is accomplished by rubbing one wing over another; in others, the sound is made by rubbing the hind legs together. Grasshoppers, crickets and katydids are notable for their ability to stridulate.

SUBSTRATE—a substance acted upon by an enzyme. As a result of the enzyme action, the substrate undergoes a chemical change and is converted into some product or products. In most cases, there is a specific relation between the substrate and the enzyme. That is, a given substrate may be acted upon only by a given enzyme or a given group of enzymes and no other.

TANGORECEPTOR—receptors that respond to touch or pressure. Tangoreceptors are abundant in the skin and muscles. Those parts of the skin that most frequently come into contact with outside objects are most richly supplied with this type of receptor. With a long bristle from a paint brush, find the areas of your skin in which tangoreceptors are most heavily concentrated.

TAXIS (pl. -es)—a turning or orientation of an animal toward or away from a stimulus. For a given stimulus, the orientation of a particular organism is always the same. A taxis can therefore be considered to fit the definition of instinct. If the animal turns or moves toward the stimulus, the taxis is said to be positive. A negative taxis is one that consists of turning or moving away from the stimulus.

THERMORECEPTOR—a receptor that is sensitive to

temperature differences. In some animals, these are extremely well developed. Certain snakes, for example, locate prey at considerable distance by detecting the prey's body heat. Mosquitoes are able to detect warm bodies and are attracted by warmth as well as by odor.

VASOCONSTRICTOR—"vaso—" refers to a vessel; in this case, a blood vessel such as an artery or vein. Such blood vessels possess a good deal of muscle tissue in their walls. When this muscle contracts, it narrows, or constricts, the passageways through these vessels. Certain substances cause the muscle to contract; these substances are called vasoconstrictors. Temperature changes may also cause vasoconstriction.

VASODILATOR—a substance that causes the muscles in blood vessels to relax, thus making larger, or dilating, the passageways through the vessels. See Vasoconstrictor.

MATERIAL SOURCES

Laboratory Supply Houses
Brom Thymol Blue
Cobalt Chloride paper
Formic Acid
Phenolphthalein
Phenylthiocarbamide paper (PTC paper)
Pet Supply or Aquarium Supply Stores
Daphnia
Supermarkets
Disinfectants
Drain Cleanser
Germicides